T0381130

STILL WATERS

A Collection of Childhood Memories

Nothing is softer or more flexible than
water, yet nothing can resist it.
--Lao Tzu

BRENDA "GIGIE" CUNNINGHAM-PARKER

BALBOA.PRESS
A DIVISION OF HAY HOUSE

Balboa Press books may be ordered through booksellers or by contacting:

Balboa Press
A Division of Hay House
1663 Liberty Drive
Bloomington, IN 47403
www.balboapress.com
844-682-1282

Because of the dynamic nature of the Internet, any web addresses or
links contained in this book may have changed since publication and
may no longer be valid. The views expressed in this work are solely those
of the author and do not necessarily reflect the views of the publisher,
and the publisher hereby disclaims any responsibility for them.

The author of this book does not dispense medical advice or prescribe the use
of any technique as a form of treatment for physical, emotional, or medical
problems without the advice of a physician, either directly or indirectly. The
intent of the author is only to offer information of a general nature to help
you in your quest for emotional and spiritual well-being. In the event you use
any of the information in this book for yourself, which is your constitutional
right, the author and the publisher assume no responsibility for your actions.

Any people depicted in stock imagery provided by Getty Images are
models, and such images are being used for illustrative purposes only.
Certain stock imagery © Getty Images.

Print information available on the last page.

ISBN: 979-8-7652-5281-9 (sc)
ISBN: 979-8-7652-5282-6 (e)

Balboa Press rev. date: 06/05/2024

CONTENTS

DEDICATION PAGE

First, I would like to dedicate this book to my younger self. My younger self gave me the material for this book. I would also like to dedicate this book to my beloved husband, Warrington. He encouraged and supported me in writing this book. He has always been my comfort. Further, I would like to dedicate this book to everyone who has played a significant role in my life.

I would especially like to dedicate this book to my mom (1925-2021). She sacrificed her life for me and my sisters. I have great respect for her strength and courage. She taught me the meaning of unconditional love. She taught me, "Bad things do happen, but how I respond to them defines my character and the quality of my life." She showed me grace.

My mom when she was raising us

My mom in her 60s

Memory, all alone in the moonlight
I can dream of the old days.
Life was beautiful then.
I remember the time I knew what happiness was
Let the memory live again.

- Songwriters: Andrew Lloyd Webber / T. S. Eliot / Trevor Nunn
Memory lyrics © The Useful Group Ltd., Faber And Faber Ltd. Gb 1,
The Useful Group Ltd

PROLOGUE

This book delves into a treasury of my childhood recollections and their profound impact on my journey into adulthood. It's a narrative inspired by the prompting of my children and grandchildren who, after my husband penned his memoir, sought to unravel the layers of my own story. Historically reticent, I've kept much of my life guarded. However, I'm compelled to unveil these formative tales, shedding light on the influences that sculpted my adult existence.

There exists a common belief that children under the age of five lack the capacity to retain memories of significant events. Yet, I stand as living testament to the contrary, vividly recalling moments from my early years. Research conducted by Carole Peterson, PhD, a distinguished professor in the psychology department at Memorial University of Newfoundland, challenges this notion. Peterson's extensive study on childhood amnesia, spanning two decades, reveals that individuals often recollect memories dating back to as early as 2.5 years old, a finding that defies the previously held belief that memory formation begins around 3.5 years old.

The anecdotes within these pages are distinctly mine, and while they may differ from the recollections of others who shared those moments, they encapsulate my truth. As Peterson aptly notes, memory is a subjective lens through which individuals perceive and retain events. Variations in memory are to be expected, and I extend my apologies if my retelling diverges from the reader's own recollections.

My childhood commenced amidst the upheaval of my parents' divorce, a period fraught with turbulence. However, upon my mother regaining custody of my sisters and me, the trajectory of my upbringing shifted towards joyous moments and cherished memories. Ironically, despite the allure of adulthood, I harbored a reluctance to embrace its responsibilities, physically and emotionally. Thankfully, fate granted me the grace of a "late bloomer."

But let's not get ahead of ourselves. Let me begin at the genesis of it all.

THE MIDDLE CHILD

GIGIE
age 1

I ENTERED THE WORLD AS THE second daughter of Clover
Geraldine Bell and Joseph Stanley Cunningham, born at Summit
Hospital, which served the Black community in Ecorse, Michigan.
Described by my mother as a serene and content infant, I quickly

won the affection of the hospital nurses with my good-natured demeanor. Despite my mother's usual reserve with compliments, she shared with me how she couldn't contain her delight in me during those early days.

As my mother prepared to leave the hospital, she faced the sudden need to name me for the birth certificate, lest I remain forever known as "Baby X." Caught off guard, she found inspiration in a comic strip character depicted as a strong, confident woman who commanded respect. Thus, Brenda, after Brenda Starr from the Detroit Times, became my official name, also honoring my maternal grandmother, Ann. Brenda Ann Cunningham became my official, birth certificate name.

However, it was my father who bestowed upon me the name Gigie (pronounced Gig-gee), a moniker that captured my perpetual happiness and laughter.

Family lore suggests that my paternal grandmother, a descendant of the Powhatan tribe, adhered to the Native American tradition of naming children based on their personality traits. This custom, deeply rooted in our ancestral heritage, led to names like Winkie, Peppie, and Puggie among my cousins, reflecting their distinctive qualities.

Despite "Brenda" gracing my birth certificate, I've always been known as Gigie, a name imbued with familial love and affection. It wasn't until later, prompted by a high school teacher's advice, that I embraced "Brenda" beyond my immediate family circle. The teacher told me I would never be taken seriously using the name Gigie. Yet, regardless of the name, I carry myself with the confidence and seriousness befitting any designation.

Within my family dynamic, I occupied the middle child role, sandwiched between two vibrant sisters. Yvonne, affectionately called Porky, was my elder by eleven months, a name bestowed by our father due to her early affinity for food. Brilliant and articulate, Porky exuded a natural eloquence and shared her knowledge eagerly.

My younger sister, Dana, arrived a year and a half after me, a vivacious extrovert brimming with energy and a love for dance and revelry. Despite my parents' divorce shortly after Dana's birth, my father had a name in mind for her: Trippy, but she was never referred to by that name.

Porky and I shared an unbreakable bond, perhaps intensified by our close age proximity, earning us the label of "Irish twins." Meanwhile, Dana gravitated more towards our mother, forming a special connection. Despite the differences in our relationships with our Mom, we remained tightly knit as a trio. While Dana shared a room with our mother, Porky and I shared a bedroom, solidifying our sisterly camaraderie.

Raised as the youngest in her family, my mother's affinity for Dana might have stemmed from a desire to provide the attention she craved in her own childhood. With Grandma's hands full raising six children as a single mother during the Depression, Mom likely sought to ensure Dana felt cherished and valued.

Although the dynamics of our family were unique, each of us felt deeply loved and cherished by our mother, who affectionately referred to us as her "three little kittens."

Mom's Three Little Kittens

Growing up, I embodied the archetype of the quiet, introspective middle child—reserved, sensitive, and deeply contemplative. One pivotal moment etched in my memory occurred when I overheard my grandmother cautioning my mother in a somber tone, "You better watch her, Clover. You know still waters run deep." This ominous warning, laden with the weight of its metaphorical meaning, insinuated that beneath my placid exterior lay complexities and depths not readily apparent to others. However, as a child, I misinterpreted this admonition, perceiving it as a veiled suggestion of danger, an unsettling notion that haunted me for years.

Yet, paradoxically, my role as the middle child brought me solace and contentment. I likened myself to the cherished filling between two slices of bread in a sandwich—the heart of the ensemble. My mother, recognizing and respecting my introverted nature, fostered an environment where I flourished. She offered unwavering support for my penchant for solitude, allowing me to retreat into the world of books even amidst social gatherings. Her gentle admonitions to others, affirming my quiet disposition and urging acceptance, shielded me from undue scrutiny.

In retrospect, I recognize that much of my demeanor was likely influenced by the early upheavals of my parents' divorce, a period marked by turmoil and adjustment. My mother, attuned to the lingering effects of these experiences, afforded me the time and space to navigate my emotions and find my footing.

As I matured, I carried forward her legacy of patience and empathy, particularly in my roles as an educator and administrator. Drawing from her example, I endeavored to cultivate understanding and support for introverted or apprehensive students, embracing their unique strengths and challenges with compassion and encouragement.

ETHNICITY

THROUGHOUT MY LIFE, I'VE OFTEN been met with the question, "What are you?" When I was young, I would look at them in puzzlement and reply, "I am a little girl." I couldn't figure out why they couldn't see that I was a little girl. It was my mother who clarified that they were inquiring about my ethnic background, affirming, "You are colored, dear." In my youth, discussions about ethnicity were rare in our family, and it wasn't a topic that occupied my thoughts.

My understanding of my heritage remained largely anecdotal until my cousin Vivian Cunningham Mason and my brother Garrett Cunningham undertook research into our paternal lineage, providing valuable insights into the Cunningham family history.

On my maternal side, stories passed down through generations enriched our understanding of our Bell-Johnston lineage, though official documentation was sparse.

Regarding my maternal ancestry, my mother conveyed that we were of mixed-race heritage, a legacy of America's fraught history of slavery and its enduring repercussions. As I matured, I grasped the profound impact of slavery's legacy, including the pervasive mixing of racial backgrounds through forced relationships.

However, my mother's knowledge of our lineage was limited to familial hearsay, with no definitive understanding of our bloodline.

On my maternal grandfather's side, Georgie E. Wilson Bell (1868-1952) was identified as black, while James A. Bell (1856–1934) was listed as mulatto in the 1930 census. On my maternal grandmother's side, William C. Johnston (1835) was purportedly of Irish descent, while Minerva E. Myers (1848) was said to have Native American ancestry.

Family lore included tales of Uncle Forest Johnston, who relocated to Oklahoma and reportedly lived among indigenous relatives, owning a hotel and bar. However, my mother consistently emphasized that these stories were steeped in familial folklore, urging caution in accepting them as factual.

For those interested in genealogy, constructing a family tree offers a fascinating starting point. My maternal grandfather, Emmett C. Bell, was born in 1890. His father, James Bell, lived from 1856 to 1934, and his mother, Georgie E. Wilson Bell, was born in 1868 and died in 1952. While the tree on my maternal side may be a bit sparse, it serves as a valuable entry point into my family's history.

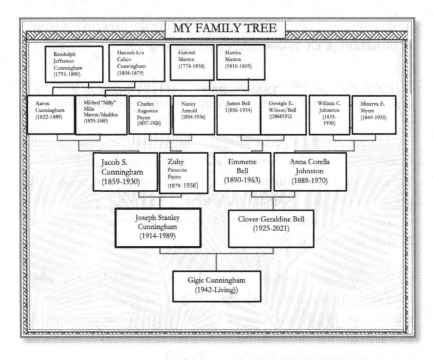

MY FAMILY TREE

Randolph Jefferson Cunningham (1791-1890)

Hannah k/a Calico Cunningham (1808-1879)

Gabriel Mattox (1778-1858)

Martha Mattox (1810-1869)

Aaron Cunningham (1822-1889)

Mildred "Milly" Milla Mattox/Maddox (1835-188?)

Charles Augustus Payne (1857-1926)

Nancy Arnold (1854-1936)

James Bell 1(856-1934)

Georgie E. Wilson/Bell ((18681952

William C. Johnston (1835-1930)

Minerva E. Myers (1849-1935)

Jacob S. Cunningham (1859-1930)

Zuby Panzetta Payne (1879-1958)

Emmette Bell (1890-1963)

Anna Corella Johnston (1889-1970)

Joseph Stanley Cunningham (1914-1989)

Clover Geraldine Bell (1925-2021)

Gigie Cunningham (1942-Living))

My maternal grandmother's maiden name was Anna Corella Johnston. (1893). William C. Johnston (1844) and Minerva E. Myers (1852) were her parents. Grandma's father, William Johnston, was born in North Carolina in 1835. His race was listed in the 1930 census as mulatto. Grandma's mother, Minerva E. Myers (1852), was listed as black in the 1920 census.

Moving on to my dad's side. Extensive research by Vivian Cunningham Mason and Garrett Cunningham revealed our ties to the Cunningham family. The Cunningham history is deeply intertwined with slavery. The uncertainty surrounding our lineage stems from whether Aaron, my great-grandfather, was fathered by Randolph Cunningham or Joseph Cunningham-- Randolph's father. Despite this ambiguity, our DNA ties are firmly established within the Cunningham lineage.

While discovering my Scottish Irish lineage through the Cunningham name was enlightening, it also brought to light the discomforting reality of slave ownership within my ancestry. Despite this, my identity has always been grounded in my African American heritage. Growing up surrounded by family of varying skin tones, I felt a sense of pride in our collective beauty and resilience.

While I may one day have my ancestry chart officially prepared, for now, I am content with the knowledge that my identity transcends any single ethnicity. As a child, I quickly learned to embrace and defend my African American identity, guided by the lessons of acceptance and pride instilled in me by my mom.

Embracing my African American heritage, despite the challenges it may entail, remains a cornerstone of my identity, a legacy passed down by my mom and cherished throughout my life.

On St. Patrick's Day one year, I decided to wear green to school, thinking that since my ancestors were Scotch-Irish, it was fitting for me to participate in the tradition. However, what unfolded that day served as a stark reminder of the prejudices deeply embedded in our society.

As I walked into the classroom adorned in green, I was met with unexpected hostility from one of my classmates. She approached me and said, "Why are you wearing green? This is an Irish holiday, and people like you aren't Irish." I was taken aback and deeply hurt by her words. In my innocence, I responded, "But I am Irish. My parents have Irish heritage because of the legacy of slavery."

The teacher intervened, placing a comforting hand on my shoulder, and explained, "St. Patrick's Day is a celebration that welcomes everyone as honorary Irish, regardless of their background."

Despite her attempt to console me, the incident left me feeling humiliated and ashamed.

From that moment on, I refrained from asserting my Irish ancestry and rejected the notion of being labeled as an "honorary Irish." The experience served as a poignant lesson about the complexities of identity and the harsh reality of discrimination.

One day, I intend to have my ancestry chart formally documented. Until I started writing this book, my curiosity about my heritage had never been particularly strong.

Growing up, my mother instilled in me a sense of self-acceptance regardless of my ethnic background. Perhaps that's why discussions about ancestry never took precedence in our household. My mother consciously avoided placing undue emphasis on our heritage. Instead, she encouraged us to take pride in our identity as African Americans, regardless of any challenges we faced, including taunts, rejections, or insults. Her teachings shaped my understanding of self-worth and identity.

My dad as a little boy
Born 1913. Died 1990

My dad as an adult

THE DIVORCE

GIGIE
Age: 4 years old

WHEN I WAS NEARLY FOUR years old, on October 29, 1946, my parents divorced, a development that deeply affected me. I was fond of both my parents and cherished our family unit; thus, their separation left me yearning for their reunion throughout my childhood.

Following the divorce, custody was granted to my father because my mother, at 22, was deemed too young to care for us. My father, 30 at the time, faced his own challenges. His job required daily attention and extensive travel, making it impossible for him to look after us during the day. Consequently, we went to live with his sister, who already had three young children. Although my aunt accepted us to please my father, her resentment toward the situation was palpable. I still vividly remember her impatience and the harsh verbal abuse she directed at us.

Life with my aunt taught me to become invisible, shrinking myself to evade her notice and anger. However, this strategy was not always successful. When she did focus on me, her words were cutting and cruel, often telling me that my mother had abandoned me because she didn't love me. Her abuse wasn't just verbal; it included forcing us to eat food left behind by her children and terrifying us with threats of putting us in the hallway at night where rats lurked

Despite the hardship, the visits from my mother were a profound source of comfort. When she discovered the extent of my aunt's harsh treatment, she was determined to regain custody. Her resolve provided a glimmer of hope in those difficult times, although the trauma of those early years lingered, influencing my behavior even after I left my aunt's home.

While I can't condone my aunt's behavior, I've come to understand her frustrations. She was overwhelmed by her own family's demands and frequently at odds with her often-absent husband.

In stark contrast, my mother modeled grace and forgiveness. She never spoke ill of my father or his family, always reinforcing our connection to the Cunningham lineage. Even when my aunt fell ill, my mother encouraged me to visit her, demonstrating her profound capacity for forgiveness and compassion.

MOM'S CUSTODY

My MOTHER OFTEN SHARED THE story of how she sought a judge who would guide her through the process of regaining custody of us. During this period, she became close to a man named David, whom she met through her sister, Bibie. David was prepared to marry my mother and support her in creating a stable home for us. With this new family dynamic established, the courts reevaluated the situation. Learning that my father, who was working in California at the time, could not provide a consistent, daily home environment for us away from his sister's care, they reversed the initial custody decision and awarded custody to my mother.

My mother's commitment to her three girls was truly remarkable. She was only twenty-two when she took us back, with our ages ranging from two to five. Despite having her own dreams and ambitions, she devoted herself fully to our upbringing, embodying a resilient and nurturing spirit.

The marriage to her second husband, David, did not last long after her gaining custody. My mother first moved us to Barnesville, Ohio, where she had been raised.

She chose to live with her mother, believing it to be a safe and familiar environment for us. This was my first memory of Barnesville, a place that soon felt like home.

Mom in Barnesville after the custody –age 22

While living in Barnesville, Porky was old enough to attend school, but I was too young to join her. My memories from that time are fragmented, yet I vividly recall that Grandma harbored strong resentment towards my dad. This bitterness unfortunately extended to Porky, who bore a strong resemblance to my dad's side of the family. It was distressing for me to witness, given the close bond Porky and I shared. Although the situation improved slightly after my mom intervened and spoke with Grandma about her behavior towards Porky, but the change was minimal. After about six months in Barnesville, my mom decided it was best for us to move back to Detroit.

My mom chose to keep the Cunningham surname, explaining that it simplified matters for us, especially since people often inquired about our father. With the same last name as ours, my mom was seldom questioned about her relationship to us. Whenever people asked about my dad, I repeated what my aunt had told me during those tearful nights: he was traveling. This seemed to satisfy their curiosity.

SHERMAN STREET

Upon our return to Detroit, we moved in with mom's sister, my Bibie and Uncle Slim on Sherman Street. We affectionately called her Bibie because as children, we struggled to pronounce Vivian. Sherman Street was part of an area of Detroit known as "Black Bottom," a predominantly Black neighborhood in Detroit, Michigan. Contrary to common belief, the name "Black Bottom" didn't originate from the racial makeup of its residents but from the dark, fertile soil described by early French settlers as river bottomland.

During that era, Black Bottom was one of the few places in Detroit where Black residents could secure housing, which was often substandard and overcrowded. Hastings Street, the neighborhood's vibrant core, was lined with Black-owned businesses, jazz and blues clubs, and nightclubs, flourishing in the first half of the 20th century. This historical insight, which I learned about later, was sourced from Wikipedia.

At the time I lived there, I was too young to appreciate the historical significance of my surroundings. I simply felt content and secure living with Bibie and Uncle Slim, which was a serene change after the tumultuous periods with my dad's sister and then my grandmother. Bibie, my mom's oldest sister, cared for us as if we were her own children. Given my mom's youth, I often playfully remarked that mom was more like our big sister, with Bibie acting as our true guardian. However, the roles were always clear: Bibie supported my mom in every way, helping her look after us, her "three little kittens."

I have fond memories of our house on Sherman Street—it was the first place I truly felt safe following my parents' divorce. We lived in a two-story flat, typical of Detroit, with living units stacked on top of each other. Bibie rented the upper flat from Mrs. Crenshaw, who lived downstairs and quickly became a cherished friend and surrogate family member. Her presence in the lower flat made us feel protected; she was our safeguard whenever we played outside.

Our living arrangements in the top flat included the large front room where I, my sisters and mom slept together in one big bed. A hallway led from this room to what served as our living room. A piano rested against the left wall of the hallway, with the stairwell on the right. Beyond the living was the kitchen, and to the left of this space was Bibie and Uncle Slim's bedroom.

This is the way the house on Sherman may have looked.

The presence of a piano in our hallway prompted my mom to enroll me in piano lessons. It's unclear why she chose me over my sisters, but perhaps it was because I was always humming or singing around the house. She prepaid for the lessons, but after the first session, the piano teacher never returned, leaving us all disappointed. With no funds to hire another teacher, my dream of learning to play the piano remained unfulfilled.

My imagination was vivid, as illustrated by an experience when I was five, playing in the pantry at our home on Sherman Street. I had imaginary playmates, tiny green beings who could hop invisibly from place to place and fit snugly in my pockets. They were always there when I needed them, helping me overcome fears, including the dread of being separated from my mom again. We played games that taught me to spell my name and discussed the books I read.

One day, my grandmother overheard me chatting with these imaginary friends and warned my mom, "Clover, you shouldn't let Gigie talk to invisible people; she could be talking to the devil." This terrified me, and I never spoke to my imaginary playmates again, nor did I tell my mom the reason.

During our time on Sherman Street, the hallway from our bedroom to the living room became a corridor of fear for me. One memorable day, my mom took Porky and me to a nearby movie theater. Misunderstanding her caution that the film might be scary, I initially found the characters on the marquee amusing. However, just five minutes into the movie, which featured Frankenstein and the Wolf Man, Porky and I were petrified. We were too scared to watch but couldn't leave until our mom returned, so we waited anxiously in the lobby, the eerie music adding to our fright.

When our mom arrived, we expressed how frightened we were. She gently reminded us, "I tried to tell you it was scary." That day,

I learned a valuable lesson about trusting my mom's judgment, a lesson so profound that I still avoid scary and suspenseful movies to this day.

The impact of that movie lingered long after. Until we moved from Sherman Street, I was terrified of the hallway, convinced that something sinister lurked behind the piano or might creep up the stairs. I needed Porky's company to brave the hallway, or I would rush through it with my eyes covered, whimpering in fear.

Despite this, I was generally happy living on Sherman Street, finding a sense of contentment in our home there.

MY BIBLE

PEOPLE IN MY FAMILY GENERALLY have tiny feet. I remember my grandmother quizzically asking my mother, "Where did Gigie get such big feet?" Embarrassed, I often hid my feet, wishing for the petite sizes that seemed a family hallmark. Grandma once boasted that she wore a size two when she married—impressive, considering I had never come close to that size. Bibie's feet were small too; she wore a size four, a size I reached at a young age. Porky had small feet like the Bell/Johnston's, while Dana and I shared the larger "Cunningham feet."

Bibie, however, reassured me that shoe size was trivial compared to one's character. She taught me, "Your outside is just a shell; it reflects what you choose to show the world. You can choose to be kind and reflect light or be harsh and cast shadows." Her words always comforted me and instilled a sense of worth beyond physical attributes.

Bibie, whose real name was Vivian, was called so because we couldn't pronounce her name when we were younger. To me, she was not just Bibie, but a surrogate mother and a beacon of wisdom, understanding, and stability. My mother explained that Bibie never had children of her own, not due to lack of desire but because she couldn't stand pain and fainted at the sight of blood. I liked to think that she had no children because, in a way, we were her children; she devoted herself to us.

Bibie was the go-to person for advice in our family, treating everyone as special and providing honest, straightforward counsel. She protected us fiercely, much like a mother bear with her cubs. After my mother regained custody of us, Bibie was instrumental in supporting us financially, often helping so my mom could manage grocery shopping. Though we moved frequently, we never strayed far from Bibie—she was both my mother's rock and my solace.

Bibie cherished hearing about our school days. Every evening, after a long day at work, she would ask, "So, tell me the highs and lows of your day," listening intently as we recounted our experiences.

I highlight Bibie in this book to demonstrate that we had more than just our mother as a positive role model. Both Bibie and Mom shared a profound value system and a commitment to instilling virtues in us.

This is way I remember Bibie always looking.

DUFFIELD SCHOOL

WHEN WE LIVED ON SHERMAN Street, I attended Duffield School, starting in kindergarten. Situated in Black Bottom, Duffield was one of the main Black elementary schools, alongside Barstow.

I vividly remember my first day of school. Having watched my older sister, Porky, go through it, I knew what to expect. But her tearful weeks of adjustment had left me apprehensive. Despite Mom's meticulous spelling drills of my full name, Brenda Ann Cunningham, I couldn't shake the nerves.

September arrived, and Mom insisted I wear my woolen snow gear over my paisley blue dress. Sweating from both anxiety and the heavy clothing, we walked to school together—my sister, Mom, and me. Each step felt weighty as we neared the imposing red brick building. My baby sister, safely at home with Bibie, felt worlds away.

At the school entrance, Porky bid me farewell, reassuring me with a wave and a shout, "You will be fine." But it was Mom's eyes I searched for confirmation. "Will I be okay?" I silently pleaded. "Gigie, I am proud of you for going to school," Mom spoke softly. She hugged me tight, her words of pride in my bravery falling flat against my rising panic.

With a forced smile, I clutched Mom's hand as we entered the building. A teacher, her face obscured because she was so tall, stood at the door and said, "Welcome, Brenda." Confusion stirred - that wasn't my name. I held onto Mom's hand as if it were my lifeline, dreading her departure.

Left alone in the classroom without my mom, I felt a crushing loneliness. When attendance was called, and the teacher's gaze fell on me as "Brenda Cunningham" went unanswered, dread gripped me. Why didn't I respond? Because my name wasn't Brenda.

Her scolding tone cut through my confusion. "Brenda, why didn't you answer?" she demanded. I glanced behind me, hoping someone named Brenda lurked there. But I was alone. Defiantly, I insisted, "I am Gigie!" and I began to cry loudly and uncontrollably.

My protests triggered chaos, and the teacher sent her assistant to summon my mom. When Mom arrived, the teacher suggested placing me in a special education class. This suggestion fueled my mom's fury. She marched to the principal's office, advocating for me. With my mom there, I calmed down and explained that the teacher hadn't called me by my name.

Later, at Bibie's house, Mom confided in her, questioning if something was wrong with me. Bibie's reassurance—"She's fine, give her time"—echoed in my mind.

That teacher's lack of understanding left scars that extended far beyond that first day.

A LITTLE
MISUNDERSTANDING

I OFTEN WONDER WHY PEOPLE CELEBRATE birthdays rather than "born days." Let's honor our parents for giving us birth. On November 5, my mom brought me into the world; it is my born day; it is her birth day and should be recognized as such.

I celebrate my born day quietly on November 5. I prefer not to have a party or any special event, as it makes me uncomfortable when someone's happiness hinges on how much I enjoy the celebration they've planned for me. In addition, I've never enjoyed being the center of attention, a sentiment I've held for as long as I can remember. A simple dinner with cake and ice cream with my immediate family suffices.

During kindergarten, I learned that my teacher spanked children on their birthdays. I found this cruel and unjustifiable. Determined to keep my November 5th a secret, I was constantly anxious she might discover the truth.

On that day, my mother suggested I wear my new lavender flower-printed dress to school, but I refused, not wanting to draw attention. Instead, I convinced mom to save the dress for later when we visited Bibie's house. I didn't confide in my mom about the teacher's practice because she always believed, "Teachers are smart and know what's best for you."

That morning, during group time, the teacher announced, "Someone in the class has a birthday today." Feeling betrayed and panicked, I was horrified when she asked, "Brenda, don't you have a birthday?" Overwhelmed, I screamed, "Please don't hit me!"

My mom was called in. The teacher explained that it was an American custom to pat children on the bottom for each year of their age. My mom clarified that I perceived this as punishment, a practice not used in our home. The teacher then suggested that I might benefit from a special needs program due to my difficulty adjusting to school.

Later that evening, at Bibie's house and dressed in my new lavender dress, my mom and Bibie discussed my sensitivity. Bibie explained that I have a literal way of interpreting situations—it was the first time I realized Bibie understood how I perceived the world.

I wish my mother had asked me directly if something was wrong. I would have assured her that there was no issue with me; it was simply a misunderstanding on the teacher's part.

Although it took me a while to adjust to school, my mom's unwavering support was a constant reassurance, helping me navigate the complexities of kindergarten.

SNUGGIES

As CHILDREN, DURING THE COLDEST days, Mom made sure we wore Snuggies to keep warm. These cozy, knitted long underpants, which stopped at the knee, were worn beneath our dresses and over our underwear. With only three pairs shared among my sisters and me, we tried to avoid the one with the stretched-out elastic waistline.

One unfortunate day, I ended up with that pair and had to wear them to school. During class, the teacher called on me to distribute some papers. I hesitated, fearing my Snuggies would slip down. Despite my reluctance, the teacher insisted. As I had feared, my Snuggies fell to the floor in the middle of the task. Mortified, I quickly stooped down, pulled them up, and sat down, refusing to continue with the papers. The teacher scolded me for my refusal and even dragged me to her desk by the arm, admonishing me for disobedience before placing me under her desk.

While being dragged, I clung to my Snuggies, crying uncontrollably. My sister Porky, who was down the hall, later told me she could hear my cries. They sent for my mom, who arrived promptly and confronted the teacher for her actions. Mom asserted her authority, making it clear that while she disciplined her children as necessary, no one else had the right to lay hands on them.

That day, I felt reassured by my mom's protective instincts. She explained the situation to the principal, ensuring that I would never have to wear the stretched-out Snuggies again without a big safety pin holding them together.

The same fury the teacher displayed that day resurfaced when she attempted to force me to stop writing with my left hand, insisting on "breaking" me of the habit. I never told Mom, thinking I was in the wrong. My family had recognized my left-handedness from an early age, attributing it to Bibie, who was also left-handed. However, the teacher's forceful insistence led me to abandon using my left hand for writing, as I was too young to defend myself.

Throughout my trials in adjusting to school, my mom remained a constant source of protection and love, demonstrating her unwavering support through her actions and strength of will.

SECOND GRADE

SECOND GRADE MARKED A TURNING point for me—it was the first time I felt that a teacher genuinely cared about my personal growth. Miss Lee, my teacher, was kind, understanding, and accepting of my shy, reserved nature. A few months into the school year, she called me to her desk and asked me to look her in the eyes. She expressed that I was special and intelligent, and encouraged me to speak up when I knew the answers. During this conversation, she mentioned the Latin proverb "Still waters run deep." I shared that my Grandma had once warned my mom about my quietness using the same words, suggesting that my silence hid many thoughts and that mom should be cautious. Miss Lee clarified that the phrase wasn't meant to be negative, explaining, "Although you are quiet, you have much to offer, and one day you will be quite successful."

The way Miss Lee framed the proverb transformed it from a warning into a compliment. She advised, "Hold your head up high and be confident." Despite the challenge of overcoming my tendency to retreat into myself, I trusted Miss Lee and strived to make her proud. Her encouragement led me to become more talkative and confident in sharing my opinions, fundamentally changing how I saw myself.

This newfound confidence was crucial when I transferred to Marcy School in fourth grade after we moved to Field Street on the east side of Detroit. The Detroit school system was crowded at the time and operated a system where students could enroll either in September or January, creating 'A' and 'B' tracks to better accommodate children's varying start times. I was supposed to start in January as a 4B student, but a mix-up on my first day placed me in 4A. The teacher repeatedly referenced material from the previous semester, leaving me confused and anxious as I hadn't covered that material.

Remembering Miss Lee's words, "Hold your head up high and be confident," I gathered my courage and raised my hand. When the teacher finally called on me, I declared, "I am in the wrong class." He calmly asked me to approach his desk, where I explained the mix-up. He then sent another student with me to the office to rectify the situation. After speaking with the principal, I was correctly placed in 4B. That experience taught me that I didn't always need my mom's intervention; I could advocate for myself. From that day forward, I learned to trust my own voice and to speak up, even to strangers.

Miss Lee's belief in me inspired me to pursue a career in education. As an adult, I followed in Miss Lee's footsteps, becoming a teacher and eventually advancing to head of school. Like Miss Lee, I became an advocate for children.

VICTORIA

*A house in Detroit similar to our house on Field
street. Our brick was tan and brown. We lived in the
lower flat. Our front door was on the right.*

Aфтер third grade, we moved further east in Detroit to
Field Street. I never knew why we moved and questioning my mom
about her decisions was off-limits. If we ever dared, she'd say, "That's
grown-up business." The new neighborhood was considered higher

status, less crowded, and safer than Black Bottom. My mom also mentioned that it had better schools.

Mom rarely had neighbors or friends over to our house. She would caution us, "Don't get close to people outside of the family because they are nosy and want to get into your business." She had one friend named Maria, whom she trusted like a sister, but I don't recall Maria ever visiting our home.

One day, a lady from my mom's workplace at J.L. Hudson's came over with her daughter, Victoria. I was immediately taken with Victoria. She had shoulder-length, dark sandy brown hair worn loose, unlike the tight braids and cotnrows most girls in our neighborhood wore, including me. Her confident and straightforward demeanor impressed me, and I remember wishing I could emulate her.

During her visit, influenced by something my Grandma once said—"Don't drink or eat after anyone, or you will catch what they have"—I thought I could literally acquire Victoria's traits by drinking from her glass. Disappointingly, nothing changed. I was still shy, and my hair remained in auburn-colored plaits.

Victoria had brought her bicycle along, and she was not only perfect in my eyes but also owned and could ride a bicycle. She offered to teach my sisters and me, but I struggled and failed to ride it. Frustrated by this and further upset by what I perceived as unfair play in a backyard game, I stormed out to the front of the house by myself. There, I saw the bicycle lying on the sidewalk. Driven by my mounting frustration, I picked it up, sat on it, and began pedaling as fast as I could. Miraculously, the bike stayed upright, and I found myself riding down the street, the breeze whooshing through my hair. The sense of freedom was exhilarating, and when I returned to where I started, Victoria and my sisters applauded my success. My anger dissolved; I had caught one of Victoria's traits after all.

That week, Mom and Bibie bought us a Schwinn bicycle. We shared it, but I used it more often than my sisters. I explored new streets and enjoyed the freedom it brought.

That experience with Victoria taught me several valuable lessons: to be resilient when things don't go as planned, to think logically rather than taking things too literally, and that persistence can lead to unexpected achievements.

One day, while riding near a private school for girls, I stopped to chat with some students during their gym class. They were dressed in gym uniforms. I learned that the school, Liggett School for Girls, was both segregated and expensive. My mom explained that attending was impossible for us, not only due to the cost but also because it was a whites-only school. However, every time I passed by, I told myself that one day I would create a school like Liggett where Black children could attend and where tuition would be affordable.

As an adult, I became the head of the Westside Neighborhood School (WNS) in California, a member of the National Association of Independent Schools (NAIS), like Liggett. Under my leadership, the school welcomed all ethnic groups, and I provided scholarships to ensure it was accessible to those who couldn't afford the tuition.

MARCY SCHOOL

Marcy School, located on the east side of Detroit, Michigan, became my educational home from the fourth to the sixth grade, and again in the eighth grade. Situated just two blocks from our house on Field Street, Marcy was a place I truly enjoyed.

My time at Marcy was profoundly shaped by my friendship with Heidi Hoffman, whom I met in grade 4A. I usually arrived at school early, savoring the quiet before the day began and recalling the encouraging words of my previous teacher, Miss Lee, about my hidden depths and potential.

One day, as I settled into class, my teacher surprised me by calling my name and asking me to join her at the back of the classroom. There, I was introduced to Heidi, a new student from Germany. She was slightly taller, with long blond braids and a distinctive hand-knitted European sweater. Despite my initial apprehension, I was intrigued and delighted to learn that I was chosen to help Heidi adjust to her new environment due to, according to my teacher, my "sensitivity and attention to detail."

Heidi's family had moved to the U.S. to escape the political unrest in Germany following the Holocaust. Her father was adamant about his disapproval of the Hitler regime and its consequences for those who opposed it. Though unaware of these broader historical contexts at the time, I came to understand through Heidi the challenges her family faced, both in Germany and as immigrants in America.

Heidi and I quickly became inseparable. She lived just a block away on Grand Blvd, and we spent countless hours at each other's homes—so much so that Bibie nicknamed her "the roomer." We shared hobbies like playing with paper dolls, board games, and making sugar cookies. Heidi also joined me and my sister Porky for Christmas caroling, a venture that became a cherished seasonal tradition.

Heidi's move away during my middle school years left a void, but the friendship had a lasting impact on my life, teaching me about the universality of human experiences despite cultural differences.

Another pivotal experience at Marcy was when Mrs. Schindler joined as the music teacher and formed a band. Heidi and I, both selected to play the clarinet, were thrilled.

Mrs. Schindler expanded my horizons beyond the classroom; she loaned me a clarinet and introduced us to classical music at the Detroit Music Hall. A weekend trip to her family's farm also opened my eyes to new experiences—jumping from a hayloft, walking through a tall tree forest, and taking my first shower instead of a bath.

In sixth grade, the arrival of Mr. Rayburn, my first Black male teacher, marked another significant chapter. While I harbored a youthful crush on him, his lessons extended beyond the science curriculum. He taught me the value of authenticity when he noticed me mimicking other girls by dragging my feet. His admonition to embrace my uniqueness was a lesson in self-esteem and integrity that I carried with me long after leaving Marcy.

These experiences at Marcy School not only shaped my academic path but also molded my personal growth, teaching me the importance of embracing my identity, exploring new perspectives, and the value of meaningful friendships.

BACK AT MARCY

WHILE ATTENDING MARCY SCHOOL, WE moved quite often, but my mom usually made sure we stayed within walking distance of the school. She jokingly referred to herself as a nomad. Apart from our house on Field Street, where we stayed for three years, we never lived in one place for more than a year and a half.

There was one exception to Mom's self-imposed decree of staying close to Marcy. When I was in seventh grade, we moved further east to Connor Street, and I had to attend Foch Middle School. It was a significant change from Marcy; I had to ride the city bus and then walk the rest of the way to school. Foch was much larger than Marcy, with a high school-like environment where we changed classrooms and teachers for each subject. I felt out of place there, knowing only my sister Porky. Four months later, we moved a short distance from Connor to Navajo Street, where I continued at Foch.

Fortunately, after seventh grade, we moved back close to Marcy, to a flat on Helen Street, directly across from the school. I was thrilled to return to Marcy for eighth grade.

Back at Marcy, I became a library assistant, a role that nurtured my profound love for reading. This passion was sparked early on by Charles, a friend of my mom's from when they both worked as elevator operators at J.L. Hudson's department store. Charles had a magical way of speaking about books; when I first met him, he mentioned he was from "upstairs," which led me to believe he might be from heaven. He brought me a treasure trove of books, including "Robinson Crusoe," "Pinocchio," "The Golden Book of Nursery Rhymes," "Moby Dick," "Twenty Thousand Leagues Under the Sea," "The Wizard of Oz," and a fascinating clown book with optical illusions. These books opened vast new worlds to me. I read them so carefully that they still looked new after many readings. I was very particular about how they were handled; no dog-eared pages or bent bindings were allowed, especially when my sisters read them.

In eighth grade, I spent every possible moment in the school library. One of my favorite books there was "Mrs. Piggle-Wiggle," known for her amusing cures for children's bad habits, such as the radish cure that motivated a dirt-covered girl to bathe regularly. I was also captivated by historical fiction. "Johnny Tremain," a novel about the American Revolution, particularly drew me in. My teacher, Mrs. Matthew, read it to our class, introducing me to the genre. After she finished reading it to the class, I checked it out several times from the library, completely absorbed by the historical narrative.

My responsibilities in the library grew over time. Initially, I helped by straightening the shelves and returning books to their proper places. Soon, the librarian, whose name I unfortunately can't recall, recognized my diligence, and offered me a job as a student assistant librarian. I eagerly accepted and took pride in my work, arriving early even on days I felt unwell. She taught me the importance of organization, loyalty, and responsibility, and made me feel valued and confident. Her mentorship and the trust she placed in me left an indelible mark on my character. I may not remember her name, but the way she made me feel—appreciated, valued, and confident—has stayed with me throughout my life.

LILA

IN EIGHTH GRADE, I BECAME best friends with Lila. Her family was unique to me, resembling the idealized white families I saw on TV shows like The Donna Reed Show and Ozzie and Harriet, but her family was Black. Lila's family was the first Black family I knew personally who lived this way. They had only two children, their home featured carpeted rather than linoleum floors, and they adhered to a regular cleaning schedule every Saturday morning. Lila's parents always communicated with loving tones and endearing names, presenting an affectionate and respectful relationship that was new to me.

Lila even dressed like the girls from those TV shows, wearing cardigan sweater sets, plaid pleated skirts, saddle shoes, and white anklet socks. Before meeting her, I hadn't seen Black families depicted in that way. Growing up in a single-parent household, and with Bibie being single for much of my childhood, I had limited exposure to affectionate relationships between Black couples. My main references for couple interactions came from white families on television, which led me to believe that such displays of affection did not exist among Black couples.

Lila introduced me to dining in restaurants—a completely new experience for me, as my mom never took us out. She taught me the etiquette of eating at other people's houses, such as not placing elbows on the table and keeping one hand in the lap while eating. I was well-versed in the etiquette of eating at someone's home but unfamiliar with the nuances of restaurant dining.

One Saturday, Lila invited me to meet her at the Big Boy's restaurant in downtown Detroit, known for its iconic double-decker burgers. Arriving before her, I found a quarter on the table and, thinking it was my lucky day, pocketed it. When Lila arrived, perfectly dressed as always, I mentioned my find. She informed me that it was a tip left for the waiter by the previous customer, leading me to feel embarrassed and foolish. I returned the quarter, and although Lila was gracious, saying it wasn't a problem, the incident left a lasting impression on me.

Reflecting on this at home, I shared the story with my sister Porky, who reassured me humorously, affirming that mistakes were part of learning. Her response helped me see that I had control over such situations and motivated me to request a cardigan sweater set and a plaid skirt for Christmas—not to mimic Lila, but to feel appropriately dressed for similar future occasions.

My time at Marcy School was profoundly transformative. Despite my shyness, I grew to be more outgoing and confident, largely because the school felt like home after so many years. This environment, combined with my experiences and friendships like the one with Lila, taught me not only about the world but also about myself, helping me to become surer of who I was and what I could contribute to the world.

STRICT UPBRINGING

MY MOM WAS VERY STRICT, singlehandedly raising three girls in Detroit. Despite having the emotional, moral, and occasional financial support of her older sister, Bibie, my mom was fully responsible for our well-being. She often reminded us, "I am the baby in the family of six, and they don't think I can raise you girls, so don't do anything that will embarrass us." It was clear who was in charge, and we knew better than to question her.

At times, Mom's strictness seemed irrational, but even as a young child, I understood she wanted the best for us and was dedicated to protecting us. I appreciated her sacrifices deeply, knowing she didn't have to fight for custody or give up her life for us, but she did. Whenever classmates complained about their parents, I'd tell them, "You should be grateful; your parents are taking care of you." I knew firsthand what it was like to live with someone who didn't truly care.

Mom wasn't one for demonstrations of affection or lavish praise. Yet, we knew of her unconditional love and high expectations. Her rule was absolute and questioning her was not an option. I learned this the hard way when I once asked if I could visit a friend and then questioned her refusal. She snatched the phone and sternly corrected my friend who dared ask "why" over the line. "Little girl, you don't ask me why; it is because I said so!" she barked before hanging up. She then turned to me, and her firm "Don't you ever ask me why again" left no room for doubt. I simply responded, "Yes, ma'am," and never questioned her again.

We had strict house rules: no sitting with adults during their conversations, no using slang or coarse language, and always behaving with proper decorum. Terms like "shoot" and "darn" were too close to curse words and strictly prohibited. Our speech was always to be respectful and proper, with adults addressed formally unless it was Aunt Bibie, who preferred just "Bibie."

Mom also enforced a strict diet, prohibiting candy and soda pop to prevent the dental woes she endured as a child.

She allowed us to play with neighbors, but only until the streetlights came on, and we were to speak properly inside the home, reserving street slang for outside play.

Mom never told us we were pretty. When others complimented us, saying we were "pretty little girls," she would respond with, "Pretty is as pretty does." She similarly never praised our intelligence. Later in life, she explained that she refrained from giving compliments because she didn't want us to become conceited. As a single mom in the city with three daughters, she believed it was safer for us to keep a low profile and avoid drawing attention to ourselves.

As a child, I took her words quite literally. If someone told me I was pretty, I doubted their sincerity, thinking they couldn't really know me or my actions, based on Mom's maxim. I internalized the idea that to be pretty meant to act beautifully, not just look it. This philosophy of not drawing attention to us suited me, as I naturally shied away from the spotlight. For my sisters, both extroverts, this proved more challenging. They found it difficult not to stand out, while I was content to blend in.

Despite my quiet and timid appearance, I possessed a strong inner drive. I was often the orchestrator behind our household's organization, especially during moves. I assigned tasks to my sisters and ensured that everything, especially the electrical appliances, were set up properly. By the first night in each new home, everything would be in place, a testament to my mom and my thoroughness.

My mom, like many parents of her generation, believed in corporal punishment. However, she rarely needed to use it on me. She said I was so sensitive that a stern look was enough to make me cry. My sisters, though, experienced it more directly. As I grew older, my punishments involved less physical discipline and more time spent standing in a corner, which I found more taxing than a quick spanking. On one occasion, after I consumed a stick of butter needed for baking, my honesty during her interrogation led to a significant time facing the wall as a punishment for eating the butter.

Financial constraints often made it difficult to secure enough food. Bibie, coming from her job, would sometimes bring money to help. Yet, there were evenings when dinner was not guaranteed. This economic uncertainty was a constant challenge, highlighting the resilience and resourcefulness required to manage our family's needs.

My mom received funds from Aid to Families with Dependent Children (AFDC), which required her to seek employment periodically due to federal mandates. The AFDC program, active in the United States from 1935 to 1997, was designed to provide financial assistance to children in families with low or no income, especially in cases where fathers were deceased or unable to work. To comply with these requirements, my mom took various jobs, including cleaning houses in Grosse Pointe, MI, and operating elevators at J.L. Hudson's department store in downtown Detroit.

Mom often said that working didn't really pay off because, after expenses for transportation and babysitters—though I don't recall ever having a babysitter—the little money left barely covered rent and groceries. Moreover, she worried about us constantly while she was at work, which led her to only work sporadically.

As a child, I developed a dislike and mistrust for social workers. Due to our reliance on AFDC, Aid to Families with Dependent Children, social workers would make unannounced visits to our home to ensure Mom was adhering to the program's guidelines. Mom was only allowed to use AFDC funds for food and rent. She was also not permitted to have a male guest over. Mom would refer to the social workers as "nosy, sneaky, interfering, prying-eyed women" because they would snoop through our closets, under our beds, and in our dresser drawers, never finding anything amiss. They also criticized Mom for moving frequently, warning her that she needed to stabilize our living situation or risk losing aid. These visits left Mom agitated and short-tempered until she could vent her frustrations to Bibie.

One particularly stressful visit from the social worker prompted Mom to make a drastic decision. That evening, she abruptly announced that we were moving to Indiana. She explained, a friend had arranged everything for us, including a home and a nearby school. He even left a car for us to drive there.

Following Mom's lead, we packed up and began our moving routine: I managed the appliances and electricity, Porky ensured nothing was left behind, and Dana assisted Mom. I rode in the front seat during our drive because I was a light sleeper and Mom needed company. We arrived to find a trailer by a freeway, intended to be our new home. However, Mom was clearly dissatisfied, and without unpacking, we returned to the car and headed back to Detroit.

Back in Detroit, we went straight to Mom's friend Marie's house. Although Marie's place was too small for us all, I overheard Mom defiantly tell her, "I will show that social worker who can or cannot move." She later admitted to us that she moved back because she didn't want to be so far from Bibie. That day, Mom secured a furnished apartment on Mack Street. By bedtime, we had settled into our new home above a bowling alley, fully set up and ready for a new beginning, as we always managed to do.

This place, noisy and imperfect as it was, allowed us to be ourselves without worrying about disturbing neighbors. Here, despite the cold nights heated only when the alley was open, we found a semblance of stability.

That episode reinforced my understanding of my mother's nomadic tendencies and gave me a profound lesson: "Home is where your family is." It's not defined by the walls that surround you, but by the people you love.

ACTIVITIES

GROWING UP, WE DIDN'T HAVE a car, so my mom, sisters, and I either walked everywhere or took the bus. I knew Detroit's bus schedules as well as a sports enthusiast knows their favorite team's stats.

About once a month, Mom would take us on a six-mile walk down Gratiot Avenue to the Family Theatre downtown for a movie. She praised our endurance and often said how remarkable it was for little girls to walk such a distance. She instilled in us the belief that we didn't need a car if we had our feet or the bus.

Despite her usual strictness and vigilance, Mom allowed me some freedom, like walking alone to the library on Burns and Gratiot, about three miles from our home. Sometimes I went with my sister or my friend Heidi, but I often ventured there by myself. Mom also let me ride the bus to the Detroit Institute of Arts and the Main Detroit Public Library on Woodward Avenue. I loved visiting the museum to see the antiquities and never grew tired of the exhibits. Reading a book was as natural to me as breathing, and I used to worry that my local library would run out of the books I loved. Visiting the larger Main Detroit Public Library reassured me with its vast collection.

Mom used to take me shopping with her because, according to her, I was quiet and didn't talk too much. She also appreciated how patiently I sat while she shopped. Although I enjoyed spending time with mom, I didn't like the shopping itself because the store was too crowded and noisy. To this day, I still do not enjoy shopping.

Mom permitted us to play with the neighborhood kids until the streetlights came on. In games like hide and seek, I would often give up my hiding spot due to anxiety; I didn't like the suspense of being found. Generally, I preferred playing less stressful games with my sisters on our front porch or skating around the neighborhood. My sisters and I were a tight-knit group, often writing, producing, and performing plays for Mom, Bibie, and a few neighbors, sometimes we included Heidi.

I was particularly good at jump rope, hopscotch, tag, and racing, excelling in soccer thanks to my speed. This contrasted with my experience in baseball, where I was usually one of the last picked on a team—until I later honed my skills. In soccer and track, especially long-distance running, my classmates eagerly chose me for their teams.

After we got a TV, we occasionally watched shows like "It's Howdy Doody Time," "Soupy Sales," "Laurel and Hardy," and "Shirley Temple," but it was rare for us. We mostly spent our time outside, or in my case, absorbed in a book.

On weekends, Mom gave us money for the movie theater. I loved musicals and often sang their songs around the house. Mom joked about always knowing where I was by my humming or singing. Mornings might find me singing "Oh, What a Beautiful Morning," and when we would move, I'd adapt the lyrics of "So Long for a While" from the television show Hit Parade to fit our leaving.

Dramatic? Absolutely, but that was simply who I was!

NO DOCTORS

AFTER GAINING CUSTODY OF US, my health became a concern for Mom as I was frequently sick with either an earache or a sore throat. When I was seven, Mom took me to a doctor to investigate these recurring ailments. The doctor recommended that I have my tonsils removed, and Mom scheduled the surgery for the following week.

On the day of the surgery, I encountered a dollhouse in the doctor's waiting room, sparking a lifelong fascination with miniature objects—from tiny dolls and furniture to my collection of miniature boxes and beaded objects as an adult.

When it was time for the surgery, the doctor placed an ether mask over my face and asked me to count backward from ten. I barely made it to five before I drifted off to sleep. Waking up from the surgery was painful; swallowing hurt and I noticed a lot of blood, which frightened me. However, Mom was there to comfort me, which eased my anxiety. Unable to swallow without severe pain, we took a taxi home, a rare indulgence since we didn't own a car.

At home, I became the center of Mom's attention. She cared for me tenderly, feeding me vanilla ice cream and Vernor's ginger ale to soothe my throat. Initially, I could only manage a teaspoon of ice cream at a time, but as I began to recover, the constant attention from Mom gradually decreased. This experience taught me that illness could bring a significant amount of love and attention, which subconsciously made me sometimes prefer being ill and staying home from school.

Despite this, my love for learning and school usually motivated me to stay healthy. Also, at the first sign of illness, Mom would administer a teaspoon of castor oil mixed with orange juice—a remedy so repulsive that it made me dread falling sick. We also took daily teaspoons of cod liver oil and swallowed cut-up garlic cloves, which Mom called the "poor man's penicillin," to ward off colds.

After the tonsillectomy, my sore throats and earaches were significantly reduced, and Mom avoided taking us to the doctor unless necessary. I didn't see a doctor again until I married my husband, Warrington.

Another health-related incident occurred when Mom and Bibie thought I was overdue for my first period. They tried various home remedies and prayers to induce it, but ultimately, it arrived on its own shortly after they stopped their efforts. This reinforced my belief that medical intervention should be reserved for more serious issues.

As an adult, I explored herbal medicine and the impact of diet on health, much to my children's chagrin. However, they were rarely sick under my care, suggesting some effectiveness to my methods.

BARNESVILLE

Dᴜʀɪɴɢ ᴍᴏsᴛ sᴜᴍᴍᴇʀs, ᴡᴇ ᴇᴍʙᴀʀᴋᴇᴅ on a journey to visit my grandparents in Barnesville, Ohio. Fondly referred to as "Grandma's house," it was nestled atop a hill overlooking a railroad station on Church Street.

*This was our view of the Railroad station down
the hill from Grandma's house.*

The two-story home boasted a facade of brown overlapping composite siding. While a small front porch adorned the entrance, it was seldom occupied, as our preferred spot for leisure was the side patio. Adjacent to the house sprawled a spacious yard, stretching both to the side and rear. In the backyard, a grape arbor divided the expanse, framing a cement walkway leading to the outhouse. Indoor plumbing was absent, save for a hand pump affixed to the kitchen sink.

At night, a "slop jar" served as a makeshift convenience for urination or defecation when venturing to the outhouse was inconvenient. Though available, I shunned its use, opting instead to wait until morning to visit the outhouse.

The backyard flourished with a sizable garden, meticulously tended by Grandma, who possessed a renowned "green thumb." Her gardening prowess extended indoors, where plants adorned every available space. Nestled to the left of the grape arbor stood a majestic sugar pear tree, yielding the most delectable, sweetest pears I have ever tasted, a sentiment that endures to this day.

Grandma's commitment to cleanliness was legendary. Her home, meticulously maintained, earned accolades from visitors who marveled, "Her house is so clean, you could eat off her floors." It was ingrained in her nature to uphold impeccable hygiene standards. She once imparted, "Even in dire poverty, one can maintain cleanliness. My children may be dressed shabby, but their attire was clean."

Mom and Porky during one of our annual trips to Barnesville.

Mom

One summer, during our customary trip to Barnesville, my mother surprised us by announcing that she would be leaving my older sister, Porky, and me in Barnesville for the remainder of the summer. While it was routine for us to visit Barnesville most summers, it was the first time I would be staying there without my mom. At nine years old, I felt a mix of nerves and excitement, a budding sense of independence coupled with apprehension.

My apprehension stemmed from memories of how Grandma had treated Porky when we were younger. Grandma had always doted on me, often declaring me her favorite because of my resemblance to my mom. Yet, Porky resembled the Cunningham side of my family. Porkey, however, being a self-professed food enthusiast, quickly won Grandma's affections with her hearty appetite. Grandma, who delighted in cooking, found joy in Porky's hearty appetite, whereas my own selective eating habits proved more frustrating to her. Porky filled the culinary gap that I left, and over time, Grandma came to appreciate her presence.

GRANDDAD

When I was young, I had an incredibly vivid imagination, often envisioning my grandad as a magical figure endowed with special powers. Surprisingly, Porky never discouraged my fantastical thoughts.

According to my mom, Grandad wasn't the best father figure to her. Allegedly, when she was just a baby, he "flew the coop," leaving my grandmom to raise six children single-handedly. I interpreted his departure as proof of his magical ability to fly. Grandma's angry remarks, like "You need to fly away, you old black crow," only fueled my imagination further.

Granddad had a distinctive physical feature, a cleft lip, which I found intriguing. At one point, I even thought it might be fun to have that separation in my own lips, imagining the practical uses, like sticking food in or using a straw. He also smoked a pipe, often placing it in the part of his lip, and would blow smoke rings through the gap.

But the true magic, in my eyes, was his ability to change his skin color. After a day of working in the coal mine, he would return home jet black. Yet, when he stepped into a galvanized wash tub, he emerged with a mahogany brown complexion. To my young mind, this transformation was nothing short of magical, although I never experienced such magic myself; I always entered the tub and left with the same color.

Granddad also wore a hearing aid, which he controlled with a box in his shirt pocket. When he wanted to tune out Grandma, he would exaggerate, turning the volume off, much to her annoyance.

Despite his flaws, Granddad showered Porky and me with love, gifts, and candies, perhaps trying to compensate for his absence during his children's upbringing. He never bought us just one piece of candy; it was always the entire carton. As we weren't allowed sweets at home, we were initially unsure how to react to the abundance of treats, but we quickly learned to enjoy them. I especially liked Bit-O-Honey. Bit-O-Honey is a bite-sized chew made with honey and almond bits.

One day, I gathered the courage to ask Granddad why he had left Grandma and his children for 12 years and how he had learned to fly. His explanation was simple yet profound. He explained that he wasn't ready to settle down. He wanted to explore the world, and the world needed to see him. So, as he watched the trains come and go at the train station down the hill from the house,, one day he decided to hop on one. From then on, he became a short-order cook for the Pennsylvania-Ohio Railroad.

Whenever we sat on the side patio in the evenings, he would regale me with tales of his adventures. Inspired, I too wanted to travel and see the world, and have the world see me. Granddad never revealed how he learned to fly; I suspected it was his own magical secret.

Uncle Sherman (my mom's oldest
brother) and my Granddad

GRANDMA

Grandma With Porky Dana And Me.
I Am On The Left.

GRANDMA WASN'T THE TYPICAL "COME-SIT-ON-MY-LAP" type of grandma. In my younger years, I didn't particularly warm up to her; she came across as gruff, irritable, and impatient. As I grew older, I realized that Grandma's demeanor likely stemmed from the trials and tribulations she endured during the Depression as a single mom raising six children . She probably didn't have much left emotionally to offer her grandchildren. Despite her rough exterior, we knew Grandma loved us and would protect us in her own way. Growing up, we understood that whichever grandchild resembled one of her children would receive special treatment and be deemed her favorite. Looking like my mom, I was one of her favorites.

Curiosity led me to ask Grandma why she took Granddad back after 12 years. However, she brushed off my inquiry, deeming it rude and asserting that it was adult business, not proper for children to discuss or even hear about.

Mom later shared that Grandma initially married Granddad against her parents' wishes. She told me that Granddad had cast a spell on Grandma with his sweet talk and empty promises. There was even a belief that he might have acquired a piece of her hair to use in a supernatural spell.

Grandma was perceived as resilient and tough, having weathered hardship, grief, and pain. Granddad's departure left her to raise three sons and three daughters single-handedly during the Depression. My mom and her siblings often shared stories of scavenging for food behind restaurants, collecting leftovers, and asking butchers for scraps and bones to sustain themselves. Beans became a staple in their diet, and rummage sales were their source for clothing. They matured quickly, learning to navigate a challenging world.

Grandma's demeanor wasn't the only aspect that intrigued me; she was incredibly superstitious, and her beliefs often rubbed off on me. I took her superstitions literally. For example, she believed that if someone obtained a strand of your hair, they could put a "spell" on you, or if a bird got a strand of your hair, you would have a headache. She also believed in the consequences of hitting someone with a broom, leaving purses on the floor, or encountering certain omens. However, as I grew older, some of these beliefs began to lose their grip on me, particularly after adopting a black cat without any dire consequences.

Grandma also believed in the presence of dead people's spirits, sharing stories of encounters with deceased loved ones. While these tales frightened me, Grandma assured us that only benevolent spirits visited her. Porkey was not frightened about such visits,, but because we shared a bedroom, Porky and I asked the spirits not to visit us.

Staying at Grandma's for the summer was a departure from city life, marked by its noise and constant activity. We traded streetlights for starry skies and embraced a slower pace. Our days were filled with roller skating, hanging out at the playground, and exploring town. We were known as "the Bell girls," reflecting our mom's maiden name, and enjoyed a sense of freedom not often experienced in the city. Our routine was simple: breakfast, roller skating, and adventures around town, only returning home for dinner.

It was a summer filled with carefree moments and cherished memories

*Grandma and Granddad in front
of their Barnesville house.*

THE HORSEWOMEN

GRANDMA WAS MISTRUSTFUL OF GRANDDAD and often accused him of seeing a "horsewoman." This led me to imagine he was seeing a woman that was part horse.

One day, after our daily outings, Grandma sent Porky and me to the hilltop gas station to check if Granddad was meeting the "horsewoman" there. I was both excited and curious to finally see her, despite being hungry and noticing the dark, stormy clouds forming.

When we arrived at the hilltop, we learned that we had just missed Granddad. Tired and disappointed, we faced the prospect of the long walk back to Grandma's house. I suggested a shortcut, and although Porky hesitated, I convinced her it was a good idea. As we started down a side street, some boys sitting on their porch yelled, "Hey, picaninny n*****s, where are you going?" I instructed Porky to keep walking and not to respond. Their taunting grew louder, hurling more racial slurs, they informed us that the street was a dead end.

Porky wanted to turn back, but I insisted we keep going. I didn't know what "picaninny" meant, but I knew "n****" was a derogatory term because Mom had forbidden us from saying it. Today, many school districts ban books containing this word, but I believe we should educate children on the history of the word and why it shouldn't be used, instead of banning books.

At the end of the dead-end road, a kind Black woman sitting on her porch greeted us. We explained our situation, and she told us the boys were ignorant and mean, advising us to "swallow your pride and turn around." Porky wanted to heed her advice, but I was too scared to face the boys again. I opted for crossing the field, even though it was freshly cut and the wheat stubbles were razor-sharp. Despite being barefoot, I persuaded Porky to cross with me. We took giant steps to move faster, but our feet soon became bloody from the sharp stubbles.

At the field's edge, we faced a deep gully with railroad tracks at the bottom. I have a profound fear of heights, but the storm was approaching, and the prospect of crossing the sharp stubbles again was too painful. Porky, with her face dirt-stained, quoted Laurel and Hardy's catchphrase, "Well, here's another fine mess you've gotten me into!" We laughed despite the situation. I felt guilty for insisting on crossing the field but turning back was not an option.

We climbed down the gully to the railroad tracks and then up the other side as the sky grew darker and daylight faded. When we finally reached Grandma's house, the rain began to fall. Grandma, visibly angry and taking the clean clothes off the line, scolded us for worrying her as a storm was coming. She instructed us to wash our feet with the garden hose, and later, Granddad wrapped our feet with gauze.

Grandma, who was terrified of storms, would make us lie on the hallway floor for hours until storms passed, warning us that any movement could attract the lightning. They had lightning rods installed on their house to protect it. A lightning rod is a metal rod mounted on a structure, designed to protect the building from a lightning strike. If lightning hits, it is most likely to strike the rod, which then conducts the electricity safely to the ground through a wire, minimizing the risk of damage to the structure.

We never told Grandma or Granddad about our adventure that day, but we shared the story with Mom and Bibie when we returned to Detroit. Grandma never asked us to go to the hilltop again, and we never saw the "horsewoman."

JOE-JOE

JOE-JOE WAS MY FIRST COUSIN and lived in Barnesville. He was the son of my mom's oldest brother, Uncle Sherman. His legal name was Joseph Lewis Bell, named after the famous boxer Joe Louis Barrow, the Brown Bomber. We affectionately called him Joe-Joe, and I harbored a childhood crush on him. My mom and grandma gently explained that such feelings toward a first cousin were inappropriate, though they never specified why, leaving me to assume it was against some unspoken law. Despite this, my feelings didn't wane—I loved him, plain and simple.

My affection for Joe-Joe pushed me beyond my usual limits. Normally squeamish around insects, I found myself catching grasshoppers to make them spit "tobacco juice," a dark, sticky substance they emit when threatened. I even let Granddaddy long-legged spiders crawl up my arm and braved climbing the pear tree in my grandma's yard despite my fear of heights. Once, I slipped and gashed my leg on a wire wrapped around the tree but refused to cry, needing to appear tough around Joe-Joe. That scar stayed with me into adulthood. My feelings could be summed up by a line from the musical Oliver! "I'll do anything for you, dear… Yes, I'd do anything, anything, anything for you."

Joe-Joe stood out from other boys I knew, both in Detroit and Barnesville. He had an independence that was magnetic; he came and went as he pleased, seemed to rule his world with a confident swagger, and always had thrilling adventures to share. He could tease my stoic Grandma and make her laugh. Hr spoke with a charming West Virginia accent, and loved the rodeo, even participating in horse and bull riding events. To me, he was a cowboy, a persona full of allure and adventure.

In our younger years, Joe-Joe likely had no idea about my deep adoration. Each time we visited Barnesville, I made sure to be near him. As I matured, I began to understand the social norms that made a romantic relationship with a first cousin impossible, but my fondness for him lingered long into adulthood.

THE FARM

In the early 1950s, my dad and his brother purchased a large property in Howell, Michigan, which we affectionately called "the farm." My uncle and Aunt Madeline, along with their six sons and one daughter, moved there from Electric Street in Ecorse, MI. My dad set up a trailer next to their house, although unlike traditional farms, there were no farm animals, just Aunt Madeline's garden.

As we got older, my mom allowed my sister Porky and me to spend time at Aunt Madeline's house in Howell. Sometimes, we stayed for a week, which likely provided us an opportunity to also see our dad, whose trailer was right next door. We weren't allowed to stay overnight in the trailer. At the time, I speculated that it might have been due to space constraints—the trailer housed my dad's second wife's three children, his third wife, and her babies—or perhaps because Mom felt more comfortable having her sister supervise us. The exact reason was never explicitly explained to us.

Visiting the farm was as delightful as my trips to Barnesville. Aunt Madeline's daughter, who was close to my age, and the constant presence of many children made it a lively environment.

My dad had remarried twice after my mom, having four children with his second wife—one of whom lived with his mother away from the farm—and six with his third, though one passed away at birth. The place buzzed with energy, and I cherished the bond with my half-sister Camille. Growing up, I enjoyed telling people I had twelve siblings, though my classmates only knew about Porky and Dana.

As an adult, after I was married, my mom remarried a man with four children. I could then proudly say I had sixteen siblings. Mom's stepchildren were quite young, and she relished being around "babies" again. The youngest, Teresa, was particularly dear to me and even lived with me for a while.

On the farm, our days were filled with adventures—we climbed hills, tended the garden, and secretly drove the tractor down the road. We enjoyed simple pleasures like making cinnamon toast and playing endlessly, darting in and out of the trailer without any strict supervision.

One visit revealed to my dad that I couldn't play baseball, a sport he excelled in and took seriously, earning him the nickname Doby after the famous Cleveland Browns player. Determined to teach me, he took me to a field the following day Initially, I would try catching the ball with my eyes shut, afraid of being hit. Through patient coaching, Dad taught me to catch with my eyes open and eventually to bat, emphasizing the need to "Keep your eye on the ball." I still remember the thrill of hitting my first ball and the rush of running to first base.

Returning to school in September, I was eager to showcase my improved baseball skills. Typically picked second to last for teams, I faced low expectations at my first time at-bat. Defying everyone's assumptions, I hit the ball and made it to first base, leaving my classmates astounded and finally gaining their acceptance.

This newfound confidence on the field was a testament to the time spent with my dad, changing my status in gym class and proving that with the right guidance, I could overcome any challenge.

HAIR

In 1983, Sandra Cisneros published The House on Mango Street, a book that profoundly impacted me. Cisneros, an American writer, is best known for this debut novel and her subsequent short story collection, Woman Hollering Creek and Other Stories. One chapter on hair from her first book resonated deeply with me, inspiring me to share my own experiences.

My mom was meticulous about our hair, insisting it be always well-groomed. She would brush and braid it every morning before school, after lunch, and again before bed, often reminding us, "A woman's hair is her crown and glory." This phrase, with its biblical roots, was deeply ingrained in us.

My sisters and I had varying hair types, affecting how we each maintained it. Porky's hair was thick, soft, and tightly curled, requiring more time for Mom to plait. Dana had softer hair with looser curls, which was less demanding. My hair was mostly soft with loose curls or straight strands, except for a patch at the top back of my head which my mom called the "bird's nest"—thick and curly. After washing, she would brush it out and apply pomade to tame the nest.

Unlike many of my friends who had their hair "pressed" with a hot comb—a common practice at the time to straighten hair—we did not. Pressing hair required avoiding activities that could make one sweat, and swimming was completely off limits. Despite not requiring my hair to be pressed to straighten it, I followed similar precautions to protect my hairstyle, becoming an excellent weather predictor to avoid humidity and rain.

In Barnesville, Grandma would coat our hair with Exceleto, a distinctive-smelling yellow pomade from a small tin jar. She used so much that it would melt under the sun and drip down our neck. It also, repelled water in the rain, making it challenging for Mom to wash out.

Once, while playing tag, a friend commented on my loose plait, saying, "You have good hair," implying it was like white people's hair. When I told my mom, she explained, "Good hair is healthy, strong hair that doesn't break or is brittle," ensuring I understood that my hair wasn't better than anyone else's.

I believed Mom's frequent brushing and plaiting of our hair was her way of keeping our hair healthy and strong.

A visit to the farm once ended dramatically when my dad decided to cut my and Porky's hair. He cut it so short that he used a razor on the neck area. It wasn't styled but rather crudely chopped. Mom was devastated when we returned home; she cherished styling our hair. She cried and scolded my dad. She was deeply hurt as if betrayed. For a long time, she couldn't tend to our hair as she had before, and we weren't allowed back to the farm.

Seeing Mom so vulnerable was a revelation; it showed me her sensitive side beneath her usual strength. It was a profound lesson that while we can't control everything that happens to us, we can choose how we respond.

ROBIN

Robin was my half-sister from my father's third marriage. When I visited the farm, I loved playing with her. One day, I casually said, "I wish I could take her home with me," not expecting anyone to take me seriously. To my surprise, Robin's mother replied, "You can take her." I was stunned. Robin was about three years old, and I was only thirteen. I couldn't believe her mom would entrust such a little one to a thirteen-year-old. I also wondered what my mom would say about me bringing a baby home. I thought Robin's mom would change her mind before we left the farm, but she didn't. Robin was placed in the car next to me, and I still thought she might return with my aunt, who was driving us home.

However, Robin stayed with me the entire week. I didn't hesitate to think I could handle the responsibility. I was determined to provide Robin with a safe, loving, and caring environment, just like the one my mom gave me—the kind of environment I longed for when I lived with my dad's sister.

I adored Robin. I was like a mama bear with her, never letting her out of my sight. She slept with me at night, we went to the store together, and she accompanied me to Vacation Bible School. We were inseparable.

One day, when I was in the bathroom, I heard Robin crying and rushed to her. I found Mom trying to console her, explaining that Robin was looking for me. Concerned, I told Mom about my worry. Mom admonished me gently, "Listen, Gigie, I raised you and your sisters; I would never let any harm come to her." Despite her reassurance, my overprotective nature didn't change.

When I took Robin around my friends, they didn't believe she was my sister. She had blonde hair and looked white. That didn't bother me. She was my "itty-bitty" sister, and I loved her deeply.

Caring for Robin taught me a lot and foreshadowed how I would be as a mother to my own children. My mom, a young but intuitive mother, instinctively knew how to care for her three distinct children, and I inherited that instinct. Watching her and mirroring what I saw, I learned to give unconditional love.

When the week ended, I was sad to see Robin go home. I wondered if her mom somehow knew that I would care for Robin so fiercely, and perhaps that's why she allowed me to take her at such a young age.

A CHRISTMAS
TREE MEMORY

WHEN I WAS ELEVEN, MY mom took a seasonal job operating
the elevator at Hudson's department store to ensure we had a good
Christmas. After a few weeks, she came home early one day, having
been fired. She recounted an incident where a little girl on the
elevator stared at her and then asked her mother, "Is that a n*****
mommy?" My mom responded to the little girl with, "No, your
mama is." She was reported to HR and dismissed. My mother was
spunky and always stood up for herself and her children. Although
I was worried about how this would affect us, I couldn't have been
prouder of her.

I learned from her to speak up for myself, a trait I carried into
adulthood, especially in protecting my children and insisting on
being treated with respect.

That Christmas, we didn't have a tree. Neither Bibie nor
Mom had the funds to purchase one. Surprisingly, a week before
Christmas, my cousin Benny Cunningham visited. We hadn't
had much contact with the Cunningham side of the family since
my parents' divorce, except through my Aunt Madeline, who was

married to my dad's brother. Benny, from my dad's older sister's side of the family, unexpectedly offered us a Christmas tree. Mom graciously accepted, and we decorated it with Benny's help. We had a tree but initially, no gifts beneath it.

We expected a few gifts from Goodfellows later. Goodfellow was a charity run by a local newspaper that provided children with fruit, candy, shoes, and clothing for Christmas. Wearing Goodfellows' shoes was somewhat embarrassing; we didn't want to seem poor, so we told kids that our cousins gave the shoes to us because they knew we loved to skate, and the shoes worked well with our skates.

A couple of days after decorating the tree, packages appeared under it even before the Goodfellows' gifts arrived. Mom explained that she and Bibie had put our gifts on layaway, making weekly payments until they could pay them off and bring them home. That Christmas, among my presents, I found a plaid pleated skirt, exactly what I had hoped for.

Mom demonstrated the importance of making Christmas special for children. Her efforts taught me that one must work tirelessly to create positive holiday experiences for their families.

I will never forget the kindness Benny showed us that day. It helped me appreciate the strong bonds within the Cunningham family.

LEAVING EIGHTH GRADE

In eighth grade at Marcy School, it was tradition for each student to sew their own graduation dress. Home economics was part of our curriculum, but by that time, we had only mastered basic sewing skills like stitching a straight seam and making an apron.

In February, all the female students were gathered in the auditorium and given a piece of white cloth. We were instructed to use this cloth to sew our graduation dresses by June 1st, with home economics classes increasing to three times a week to assist us.

I was immediately concerned. Sewing a dress seemed daunting, especially since all my sewing had to be done at school; we didn't have a sewing machine at home, and my mom didn't sew. Many of my classmates mentioned that their mothers would either help significantly or practically sew the dress for them. My friend Lila was among those expecting substantial help from her mom.

During our first intensive home economics class, I focused on perfecting the straight seam, but my confidence waned when one of the girls accidentally sewed through her finger with the machine needle. The next lesson involved cutting out our dress patterns. While some girls had their patterns precisely cut by their mothers at home, my initial attempt was uneven, although the teacher helped me correct it. I felt it was unfair that some girls received so much help—it seemed equivalent to having someone else take your final exam.

My mom had always taught me the value of fairness and truthfulness, expressing pride in my honesty, even if it led to trouble. Thus, the situation with the dresses struck me as fundamentally wrong. If the assignment was intended to teach us to sew, then everyone should have been doing their own work.

When I shared my feelings with my mom, her response was a life lesson. "Don't ever say something isn't fair. It is what it is," she said. She illustrated her point with her own experiences, like being fired for confronting racism at work, or our financial struggles. She taught me to focus on doing what was right and doing my best, regardless of the circumstances.

Following her advice, I completed my dress on my own. It wasn't as polished as those made with parental help, but I wore it with pride to my eighth-grade graduation—and never again after that. From my mom, I learned the value of perseverance and gratitude, lessons that have stayed with me throughout my life.

HIGH SCHOOL

AFTER GRADUATING FROM THE SMALL, safe environment of Marcy School, I faced the transition to high school. My mom, who herself had only completed eighth grade, was determined that my sisters and I would graduate from high school. This was not just a hope but a firm goal, reflecting her belief in the importance of education—a dream she had to forego to focus on raising us.

I began ninth grade at Eastern High, located at Mack and Grand Blvd. in Detroit. After completing ninth grade there, our family moved to Southwest Detroit, and I transferred to Southwestern High where I enjoyed playing the clarinet in the school band. The band helped me integrate and meet more students. However, after only four months, we moved back to the East Side of Detroit, and I returned to Eastern High to complete the first half of tenth grade.

Our next move was abrupt and far-reaching—we relocated to Indiana. But the stay was brief; we were there for just a day before returning once again to the East Side of Detroit. Overwhelmed by the idea of returning to Eastern High after multiple farewells, I resisted going back, feeling too embarrassed by the repeated departures and returns. When I expressed this to my mom, she firmly stated that not attending school was not an option, prompting my unexpected request to attend Catholic school—a decision inspired merely by passing a Catholic church on my way to the library, despite having no personal connections to Catholicism.

Unsure, but open to exploring my request, my mom walked with my sisters and me to a Catholic school named St. Charles, about five miles away. It was a cold January day, and the long walk was arduous. Upon arrival, we learned that we were not in the correct parish and that there was a closer school we could attend. The walk back was just as taxing, and despite feeling guilty for the inconvenience to my family, my resolve to not return to Eastern High was unwavering.

After discussing it further at home, and refueling with a peanut butter and jelly sandwich, we visited the nearer Catholic school, St. Catherine's, which was in our parish. Here, we were warmly received by the Mother Superior who confirmed we could enroll. Facing financial constraints, my mom explained our inability to afford tuition and uniforms. Impressively, Mother Superior arranged for uniforms and offered my mom a job at the convent to help cover the costs, ensuring that we could attend.

I started at St. Catherine's in what was technically still my tenth-grade year due to their different academic structure. I was given the choice to advance to eleventh grade or remain in tenth; I chose to stay in tenth grade. I appreciated the smaller, more intimate setting compared to Eastern High, with its fewer classrooms and just a single hallway of rooms. This environment, coupled with daily church attendance, resonated deeply with me, enhancing both my spiritual life and my commitment to education. When I matriculated to eleventh grade, I officially joined the church, drawn by the serene environment and the teachings about the saints.

This period of my education not only aligned with my mom's aspirations for us but also marked a significant chapter in my personal growth and academic journey, underscoring the profound impact of parental support and the unexpected paths that lead to fulfilling one's educational goals.

My graduation picture
from St. Catherine's

WARRINGTON

I BELIEVE MY DISCOVERY OF ST. Catherine's school was in divine order. Before that providential day of my enrollment, I knew nothing about Catholics.

While attending St. Catherine's, I became acquainted with my future husband, Warrington.

Dana, my sister, was friends with Warrington's sister, Eugenia. One day, Dana wanted to participate in the school's football game, but as usual, Mom wouldn't let her go without me. We always had to accompany each other. I reluctantly went along. When we arrived, Warrington, Eugenia's brother, was home from college and at their house. His dad drove Warrington, Eugenia, Dana, and me to the game. Warrington and I did not speak at the game, but he drove us to an after-party at one of Dana's classmates' houses.

When we got out of the car, Warrington looked at me and asked if I wanted to go to a nightclub. I thought he was showing off because he was in college. First, I was not dressed for a nightclub, and second, I was underage, which he knew. My sister Dana responded, "I will go with you." I quickly added, "He asked me." I was calling his bluff by answering affirmative.

As it turned out, he took me to get pizza. I liked him because he was polite, and we conversed intelligently. He seemed to defer to and respect my opinion on the subjects we discussed, even though he was a college student.

That evening was the beginning of our relationship. He went back to college, and we corresponded by mail. When Warrington came home for his Thanksgiving break, he invited me to his family's house for Thanksgiving dinner. He picked me up in his car, and on the way, he told me, "I am going to marry you." I thought he was bluffing again, so I replied, "Uh-huh." Four years later, we were married. Again, divine providence.

Warrington later told me that he first saw me in church before he ever saw me at his house. We both attended early morning mass. He mentioned that he had wondered how he would meet me because he couldn't find me after morning mass. I used to leave church immediately after communion and run the block to my house, which is why I never saw him there.

As of the writing of this book, Warrington and I have been married for sixty years.

My wedding day.

SPIRITUALITY

ONE CONSTANT IN OUR NOMADIC lifestyle was my mom's insistence on finding a church in each new place we moved. Although she didn't always join us, she made sure we attended every Sunday, and more often if we joined the choir. Porky usually sang in the choir, and I went along to practices. I was too shy to join. Every time we joined a new church, I was baptized, believing it necessary to become part of the congregation. Over the years, I underwent baptism across various denominations—Baptist, Episcopalian, Lutheran, Methodist, Pentecostal, Nazarene—before finally embracing Catholicism in high school after enrolling at a Catholic school. It was there I learned that baptism need only be done once.

My belief in a higher power has been with me as long as I can remember. I've always sought a deeper connection with something greater than myself. When my husband asked why I was drawn to spirituality, I answered, "I believe there is a purpose and meaning to everyone's life. Exploring spirituality helps me become better acquainted with a higher being and understand myself more deeply."

I've learned that it's crucial to recognize spirituality as a profoundly personal experience; not everyone will feel the same connection to it.

Negative experiences with organized religion, alternative sources of fulfillment and meaning, cultural influences, personal beliefs, and life experiences all shape an individual's spiritual journey. It's vital to respect each person's unique perspective on spirituality.

My mom instilled in me the belief in a higher power and the importance of attending church to seek inspiration and guidance each week.

NAZARENE CAMP

My mom, teachers, and other adults always perceived me as quiet and dutiful, but that changed one summer at Nazarene Camp.

One summer, I was surprised when my mom allowed me to join my cousins from the Cunningham side of the family at summer camp. As I grew older, mom became more lenient about my interactions with the Cunninghams'. They were a part of my family I was eager to know better. Having always harbored a longing for my absent father, any connection to his family felt significant.

That week at camp was transformative. I shifted from a reserved, compliant child into an independent, rebellious individual. I relished my newfound freedom, defying the counselors' instructions and enjoying the sense of control. It was a way to compensate for earlier years when fear of abuse had kept me strictly adhering to my aunt's expectations, with little say in my own life.

I vividly remember one incident. At camp, I bonded closely with my cousin, and we mostly kept to ourselves. One day, we were told that we had to make friends with other campers. In response, my cousin and I devised a clever strategy that allowed us to follow the counselor's directive while also preserving our close bond. When the counselor threatened to send us home for not mingling with others, we proved her wrong by demonstrating that we had forged friendships with almost every bunkhouse. It was a triumphant moment that unveiled my persuasive leadership skills.

That summer was a revelation. I realized I didn't need to conform to others' expectations to be liked. The world would keep turning even if I didn't follow all the rules. It dawned on me that I possessed latent strengths and leadership potential, qualities that were nurtured at home but now validated among strangers.

Beyond personal growth, I cherished the camp experience for other reasons. I discovered the art of weaving, sparking a lifelong passion that led me to pursue a master's degree in fine arts with a focus on weaving and fibers. Additionally, I developed a fondness for breakfast cereals beyond oatmeal and cream of wheat, enjoying the likes of *Snap, Crackle, Pop, Shredded Wheat, Raisin Bran*, and *Cheerios*.

Due to its religious nature impression on me. I savored the nightly church services, captivated by the biblical tales and the soul-stirring music.

In retrospect, that summer camp was a defining moment. It revealed my inner strength and affirmed the depth of my character, knowledge, and emotions. I embraced the notion that "still waters run deep," recognizing the richness within me.

Additionally, spending time with my cousins on the Cunningham side was a highlight, deepening family bonds that were precious to me.

A LETTER TO MY YOUNGER SELF

In this final chapter, I would like to share a letter to my younger self, offering the insights and reassurances that only time can provide.

Dear younger Gigie,

I want to assure you that everything turned out wonderfully. You have been blessed beyond your wildest dreams, and every experience and challenge you've faced has shaped the fulfilling and successful life you lead today.

Despite the emotional and physical abuse, you endured as a child, it's important to recognize that not everyone who experiences such trauma develops long-term mental health issues. I believe it was your mother's unwavering dedication to providing a safe, stable, and nurturing environment that played a pivotal role in your healing process. Additionally, the constant presence and guidance of God have been instrumental in watching over your well-being.

Your demeanor as an adult is quite different from your younger self. While you still feel shy and uncomfortable around unfamiliar faces, you exude assertiveness and confidence in your professional setting. Your colleagues view you as kind yet firm, self-respecting, and inspiring. Initially, some may perceive you as aloof, but they soon come to appreciate your good humor, agreeableness, and graciousness.

If I could offer advice to you, my younger self, it would be to take Miss Lee's counsel to heart. Look people in the eye, trust in the inherent goodness of humanity, and be open to new experiences. Remember how she described you as "still waters," reflecting your depth of character, knowledge, and emotion. These traits will become your strengths, allowing you to face life's challenges with calmness and thoughtfulness.

Though Mom may have seemed overbearing at times, her intentions were always pure. She wanted nothing more than for her daughters to be happy, loved, safe, and secure. Raising three girls alone in the city, under financial strain, was no small task. Despite the hardships, you all managed to stay out of trouble, avoid teenage pregnancies, and fulfill her wish of graduating from high school. Your further academic achievements, including a Master's Degree, are a testament to both her sacrifices and your resilience.

Gigie, you'll find this quite fascinating. In your journey to deepen your spiritual understanding, you enrolled in a study course. At the conclusion of this course, you were assigned a spirit name, believed to represent your higher self. The name given to you is Baekdu San. Baekdu Mountain, home to one of the highest crater lakes in the world known as Heaven Lake (Lake Cheonji, 천지, in Korean), straddles the border between North Korea and the Manchurian region of China. This sacred site is revered by both Koreans and Chinese and stands as the most majestic mountain lake in Korea, located in the northern part of Samjiyon City, Ryanggang Province.

So Gigie, it seems you've come full circle—from being likened to "still waters" in your youth to embodying Baekdu Mountain, Heaven Lake, as an adult.

Your journey to success is truly remarkable. Graduating with distinction from the University of Michigan and later earning a Master's degree from Carnegie Mellon are significant accomplishments. Your career in education, spanning various public and private schools and culminating in leadership roles, demonstrates your dedication and expertise.

Your marriage to Warrington Parker also stands out as a cornerstone of your personal achievements. Warrington has been a supportive and loving partner, helping you overcome shyness and insecurity. Together, you have raised four successful children who have excelled in their respective careers, spanning law, academia, and healthcare.

While your childhood was characterized by frequent relocations, your adult life found a more stable rhythm, punctuated by moves related to Warrington's career advancements. Each relocation brought its own set of challenges, but also opened doors to new growth opportunities and adventures. Your decision to settle in Chelsea, MI, was particularly impactful, offering your children a slice of rural life along with valuable lessons in hard work and responsibility.

Fueled by the tales your Granddad shared, your lifelong desire to travel turned into a reality. You've journeyed across Europe, enjoyed the islands of Hawaii, wandered the streets of Brussels, explored the vast landscapes of China, and more, fulfilling a dream you've cherished since your youth.

So, Gigie, rest assured that you have been blessed abundantly. You need not worry about any situation because everything has ultimately worked out for the best. Embrace each day with gratitude and confidence, knowing that you are truly "blessed beyond your fondest dreams."

With all my love and the wisdom of hindsight, your older self

P.S. Gigie through all your trials and tribulations, you learned, *"I am not what happened to me. I am what I choose to become"*. –Carl Jung.

Gigie, first trip to Barnesville

ABOUT THE AUTHOR

Brenda "Gigie" Cunningham-Parker

Gigie, (pronounced "Gig Gēē"), graduated with distinction in Education from the University of Michigan and earned an MFA in fibers from Carnegie Mellon University in Pittsburgh, PA.

After completing her BA, Gigie taught in public and rural schools in Michigan, as well as private independent schools in Pittsburgh, PA, and Palos Verdes Peninsula, CA. She was passionate about teaching and always saw herself as a child advocate. Following her move to California, where her husband transferred to work for the Rockwell Corporation, Gigie joined Chadwick School. After five years of teaching at the Village School (K-6), she was promoted to Curriculum Director and later became the Head of the Village School, serving in that role for three years.

Gigie subsequently accepted a position as Head of Westchester Neighborhood School (WNS), later renamed Westside Neighborhood School, in California. During her tenure at WNS, she fostered a child-centered, diverse student body and a supportive school culture.

After serving thirteen years as Head of WNS, Gigie resigned in 2007 to collaborate with her husband on projects aimed at enhancing parental involvement and student learning.

In 2009, Gigie and her husband were invited to aid in revitalizing the struggling African-centered K-8 Detroit Public Charter School, Timbuktu Academy of Science and Technology, which was later renamed Obama Leadership Academy. Their leadership over four years led to the school receiving a five-year extension of its charter, credited to a highly motivated and dedicated staff.

Gigie has co-authored several articles with her husband, participated in his projects at the United Nations in New York, and traveled to South Korea to engage in Brain Education events, training teachers and students on its benefits.

Now, Gigie is enjoying her retirement with her husband on a golf course in Sedona, AZ.

Printed in the United States
by Baker & Taylor Publisher Services